Your name

1

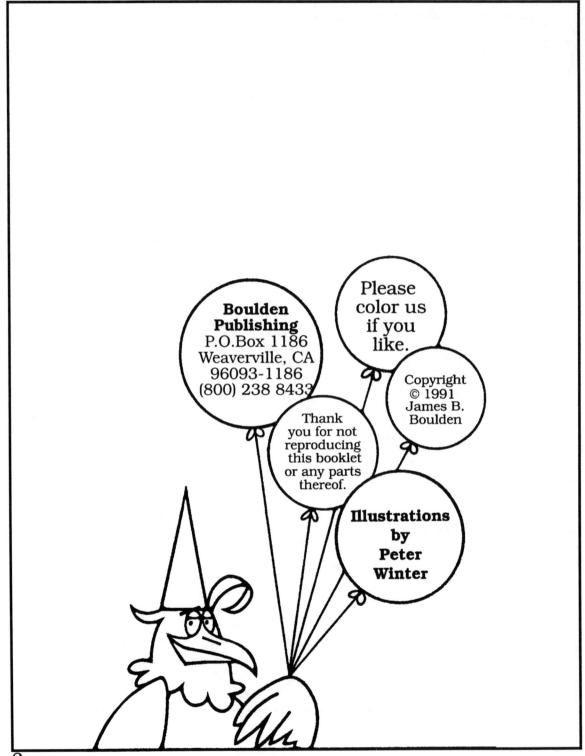

Printed in USA

Please draw a face showing how you feel about discussing divorce.

3

I n the beginning, each of us has one mom and one dad.

These are our natural parents. They belong to us forever.

One reason that families break up is that people change.

Parents sometimes change, how they feel about each other.

Sometimes parents stop loving each other and find it hard to live together.

They may argue and do things that hurt each other.

There is nothing that kids can do to stop this.

Life can become very unpleasant for kids when their parents fight.

Do you ever feel like running away?

Mom and dad may shout at us when they are upset.

They may do this even when we have not done anything wrong.

*Do you ever feel that it's your fault that your parents fight?*_____

Why do you feel this way? _____

_____

_____

Kids can't <u>FIX</u> the problems between Mom and Dad because they don't <u>CAUSE</u> the problems.

Grown-ups get married and divorced for grown-up reasons — not because of what kids do.

Parents have to work things out for themselves.

Kids cannot keep their parents together. Begging does not help.

Even if kids promise to be very good — it does not make any difference.

Kids have to accept divorce no matter how much it hurts.

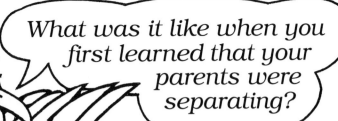

What was it like when you first learned that your parents were separating?

My first thought was _____

_____

The first person I told was _____

_____

I felt sad because _____

_____

I felt mad because _____

_____

I was afraid because _____

_____

I was glad because _____

_____

I worried about _____

_____

_____

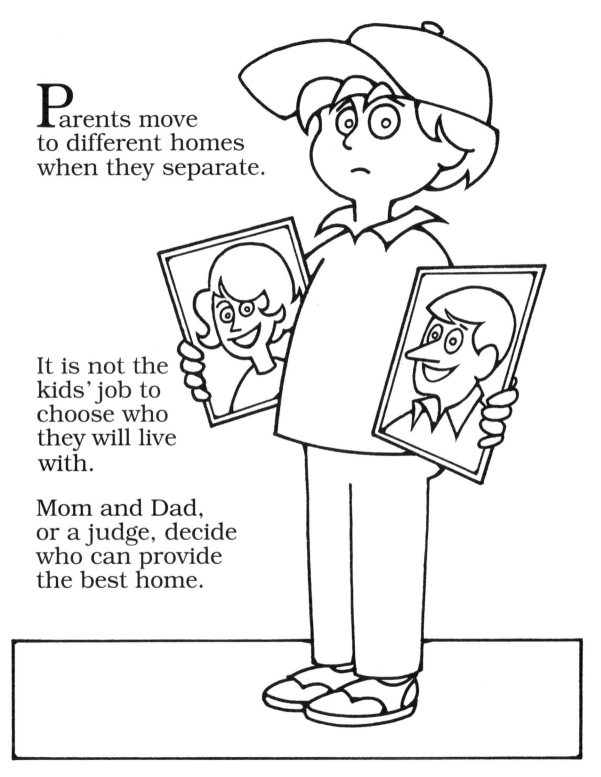

Parents move
to different homes
when they separate.

It is not the
kids' job to
choose who
they will live
with.

Mom and Dad,
or a judge, decide
who can provide
the best home.

One thing for sure is that you will grow up with a place to live and someone to care for you.

Who do you live with today? _____

_____

How do you feel about living there? _____

_____

_____

Kids often move to a new school when parents separate.

Have you changed schools? _____

What is the name of your new school? _____

How are you doing in school? _____

What are the names of your friends? _____

Have you changed where you live? _____

Do you miss your old home or school? _____

It is not always possible for brothers and sisters and pets to all stay together after a divorce.

It is very difficult for one parent alone to take good care of several children.

Are you separated from your brother, sister or a special pet you love?_____

How does that feel?_____

_____

_____

Draw a picture of the toys or pets or friends that keep you company.

You may live part time in two different homes after your parents divorce.

This is a chance to spend time alone with each of your parents.

They may be more fun to be with after they separate.

You will feel more at home when you have clothes, special toys and your own space with each parent.

Mom and Dad may stay angry
after they separate.

They may even say mean things to you
about each other.

It is OKAY to ask them to stop that.

You don't want to hear anything bad
about either parent.

What would you like to say to your parents about their separation or divorce?

Your divorce makes me feel _____

_____

_____

I wish _____

_____

_____

_____

It would help if _____

_____

_____

_____

Please don't _____

_____

_____

_____

Mom and Dad may divorce each other, but they will never divorce you.

You will always be their child...

...and they will both love you forever.

"Divorced" means "no longer married."

Mom and Dad may start to date new friends.

It is sometimes hard to see our parents with strangers.

When divorce happens, it is okay for kids to feel angry, happy, afraid, worried, sad or any other way.

It helps to share these feelings with people who care and will understand.

Who do you talk to about your feelings?

_____

_____

List two things you would like to say.

_____

_____

Children with divorced parents are not different or alone.

There are many kids with the same experiences.

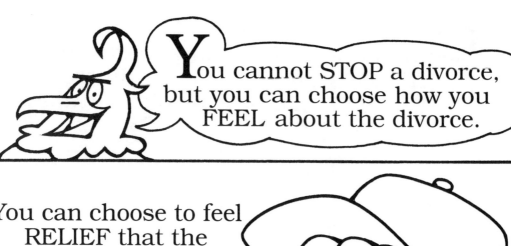

You cannot STOP a divorce, but you can choose how you FEEL about the divorce.

You can choose to feel RELIEF that the fighting is over.

You can choose to be HAPPY that Mom and Dad feel better living apart.

You can have as many different feelings as you wish.

How do you choose to feel?

_____

Divorce is an end to living in an unhappy home.

Divorce is also a beginning — the start of a new life.

Good things often follow after parents separate or divorce.

It just takes time for hearts to heal.

RESOURCES FOR CHILDREN IN DISTRESS
Used by 25,000 Institutions   One million books in print

ACTIVITY BOOKS

Age appropriate materials featuring ethnic and gender diversity are available for children from kindergarten to Sr. High School.

**AIDS Awareness ● Anger Control ● Bully / Victim ● Bereavement
Blended Family ● Communication ● Conflict Resolution ● Divorce
Feelings Awareness ● Foster Families ● Friendship ● Illness
Peer Pressure ● Physical Abuse ● Remarriage ● Self-esteem ● Sexual Abuse
Single Parent ● Substance Abuse**

REPRODUCIBLE ACTIVITY PAGES

Low cost consumable companions to the **Activity Books**, the **Activity Pages** contain all of the exercises and most of the graphics from the corresponding activity books in an easily reproducible 8 1/2" x 11" format. Now at minimum expense, each child can have their own materials to mark up and take home to discuss with their parents. The Reproducible Activity Pages are available in both English and Spanish Languages.

SUPPORTIVE MATERIALS

A broad range of supporting materials are available including CD ROMs, Videos, Role-Play Kits, Small Group and Classroom programs, projection activities, parent guides, Draw-A-Face packs, Feelings Posters. Puzzles and games bring laughter and excitement to the counseling process. Emphasis is on child involvement and participation.

PHONE FOR FREE CATALOG (800) 238-8433

BOULDEN PUBLISHING
P.O.Box 1186, Weaverville, CA 96093-1186